CORNISH SAINTS

AND

HOLY WELLS

HELEN FOX

VOLUME ONE

THE STORIES OF THE SAINTS

THE LOCATION OF THE WELLS,

AND

THE DIRECTIONS TO THEM

Copyright ©Helen Fox 2016

Paperback ISBN: 978-1-910088-40-1

Ebook ISBN:978-1-910088-45-6

Published by SifiPublishing 2016

SIFIPUBLISHING

WWW.SIFIPUBLISHING.CO.UK

Pv11

I wish to thank those who have shared some of the journey with me in my search to discover some of the Holy wells of Cornwall.

The Crones group, for their encouragement and continuing support.

To all the authors of previous works and writings about the Holy Wells.

The legends, myths and stories of ancient Cornwall and the Saints which were my inspiration. (See Bibliography)

My family and friends.

Volume One of 'Cornish Saints and Holy Wells'.

In early 2014, I produced an original set of 63 oracle cards based on some of the Holy wells. (Available on Amazon)

I was then asked to produce a book about the stories of the Saints and the wells, used for the oracle cards. People also wanted to know directions to the wells and these are included in this book.

There are thought to be over 400 wells and springs in Cornwall, and I have visited many of them. Some are lost due to neglect, building works, weather and geological conditions, but there are still many to enjoy. All are very different in their own ways, and have different uses, histories and energies.

"There are more Saints in Cornwall than there are in Heaven"

Index

CORNISH SAINTS
AND
HOLY WELLS

1-Alsia Well

1-Alsia Holy Well, St Buryan

Feast day of St Buryana= 4ᵗʰ November

St Buryana was a Celtic saint, and daughter of a chieftain, who came from Ireland and was known for her healing abilities, especially in cases of paralysis, and for the healing of children with rickets. In the 8ᵗʰ century the son of King Gereint of Dumnovia (the name of the country of Devon, Cornwall and Somerset) was cured of paralysis after praying to her for healing.

The well would have been used for divination and as a wishing well, especially during Beltane, traditionally on the first of May, when young girls are looking for love. After dropping a pin or pebble into the water- the number of bubbles would indicate the number of months or years she would need to meet her true love.

The well has such a lovely feel, and the water in the well is cool and clean.

Nearby is The Merry Maidens, whose stones form a perfect circle, near two Celtic crosses.

Location- SW 393 251

The well is on private lands, Lower Alsia Farm, but the owner is happy for folk to visit and has allowed the well to be used for ceremonies, rituals and celebrations. Take the B3283 to St Buryan and go through the village and take the next turn on the right towards Sennan. Just past the Mill house there is a lay-by on the left for parking. Go over the style and a path leads across the edge of two fields and down to a stream where the well is located in the hillside.

"My waters are clear and fresh to cool the ardour of the young. At Beltane we look for love and joy in a special other, and the maiden will do the choosing. After dancing and singing and being joyous in the beauty of the time of year: the first day of summer is 1ˢᵗ May when we celebrate and speak our wishes and desires"

2-St Anne

2-St Anne Holy well

Feast day= 26th July

Anne married Joachim and is the mother of Mary, and so the grandmother of Jesus.

St Anne is the patron saint of grandmothers, single women and of women in labour. She is sometimes also associated with cabinet makers and her symbol is a door.

Location: - SX263 985

On the B3254 road between Launceston and Stratton lies Whitstone, so follow signs to the church at the top of the village.

The well is to be found in the grounds of the church. At the end of the entrance path, on the left of the church is a handrail down a grassy slope. The well is in the bank on the left and has been well looked after, and vegetation cleared. It has a very interesting carving of a female head into the back wall- obviously a representation of the Goddess, and a very powerful image.

"The water from my well has many purposes especially welcoming the new life into the world. Baptism is to provide safety and guidance to the young on their spiritual journey this life-time. From ancient times of the goddess this has been our role"

3- St Bryvyth Holy Well

3-St Bryvyth Holy well

Feast Day- 14th October

She is also known as Brevita- she is one of the daughters of King Brychan, but otherwise nothing is known about her.

The local church is dedicated to Saint Manachus but what the connection between the two is is not recorded.

<u>Location-SX078 590</u>

Take B3269 to Lanlivery and park in the car park of The Crown Inn. Follow the footpath to Luxulyan which is near the inn to the north. Not far down the path on the left, about 20-30 yards, is a gate leading into a garden. Skirt around the pond and over a small bridge. The path leads to the well which is tucked into the bank by the stream. The place transports you to a magical realm.

"Listen carefully and you will hear voices singing their special songs, of the mysterious ways of saints and teachers, leading you to realms of wisdom and the old knowledge. The waters from this well will connect you to Mother Earth energy."

4-St Cleer Holy Well

4-St Cleer Holy well

Feast day=4th November

The well is dedicated to St Clare-St Cleer is actually the name of the village. She was stalked and murdered for spurning a local chieftain, who did not take rejection easily.

The well water was used ceremonially as it flowed to a Bowsenning pool for people with mental health problems, when they would be dowsed in the healing waters, hopefully to cure their emotional afflictions.

The well was restored in 1864 and like a lot of the wells that have been repaired; there is a metal grill over the waters which flow into the sunken well.

Next to the well- house there is a lovely ancient Celtic cross engraved with Ogham characters.

Location-SX249 683

From Liskeard in south east Cornwall, take the B3254 towards St Cleer, Minions etc and at the Y junction bear left. Go along Fore St and take the first right turn, into Well Lane towards Tremar. The well is on the right before the school.

"For many years my waters were used to combat the illnesses and grief of the local folk who lived lives of great poverty and hardship. The moors can be a place of extremes with deep dense mists descending without warning very quickly. It is easy to become disorientated and confused and to wander into bogs and gullies which can induce great fears of drowning and being buried alive"

5-St Clether

5-St Clether Holy well

Feast day= 13th November

St Clether- his name means 'the Aged', was a son of King Brychan. His bones are said to be buried in a recess in the chapel, and as the water passes over them, absorb the gift of his blessings.

Location-SX203 847

From A395 take any road to the village. Park outside the church and the path to the Holy well and chapel runs along on the left. Go through the gate and follow the path across a field for about ¼ mile. The chapel is one of the largest in Cornwall and has the original altar stone. The water from the well runs through the chapel below the altar and out into the receiving bowl outside. (The only other chapel with this is Dupath in Callington)

This well is set in the lovely Inney valley, and has a beautiful chapel next to it which has been lovingly restored. It is thought that the foundations of this chapel are thousands of years old. At one time the floor of the chapel was lowered to enable the water to flow through and out of the chapel.

"I invite you to use this space and chapel for ceremonies, celebrations and festivals. I offer a peaceful and protective atmosphere for worship and appreciation. The presence of 'the guardians' in the rocks above will keep you safe always while you are here."

6-St Cyors Holy well-

6-St Cyors Holy well

Feast day= 17th May

This well is now dry since the railway was built in 1890, so it doesn't have the same magic as the wells and springs that are still a source of pure, clean water.

St Cyors is the 3 year old child of St Julitta (her well can also be found at Lanteglos and Boscastle), who was killed in front of his mother, as he became the youngest Christian martyr. (no. 48, St Julitta Holy well)

Location- SX054 580

Take the A390 through Lostwithiel towards St Austell and take any of the turnings on the right to Lanlivery. Go through the village and follow the road to Luxulyan. It can also be approached from the Bodmin direction by taking the A30, turning left onto the A331 towards Bugle. The turning to Luxulyan is a short way along the road on the left. Luxulyan is dedicated to St Sulian.

In the main street the well remains are in an enclosed paved area on the right. Local folk keep the site clean and tidy and have planted flowers around the site, which is paved with a wall around the enclosure.

"Look to your mothers. The Great Mother who holds us all in her embrace.

Your birth mother who has held you in her body until you were ready to enter this world.

The other mothers who share your experiences and give you comfort and advice and support.

Remember with love and accept"

7- St Euny Holy Well

7-St Euny Holy well

Feast day= 1ˢᵗ February (which is Imbolc -a time when the sleeping dragon raises from its slumbers)

St Euny is an important saint in west Cornwall (see No 38)

Location – SW691 413

From the A30 take a right turning to Sancreed. Head left towards Grumbla and follow signs to Carn Euny Settlement. It can also be approached via Brane but this is a longer walk from the parking area. As you enter this ancient village there is a gap in the hedge and a gate, which leads to the holy well of St Euny. There is often a removable metal gate across the entrance. There are several steps down to the water which is cold and clear and has a reputation for its healing properties, especially of children.

In the settlement there is a lot to see particularly the fogue and central circular room. It is so easy to imagine ancient rites and rituals taking place here.

8- St Cuby Holy Well

8-St Cuby Holy well

St Cuby or Cybi, was the son of St Selevan and a true Cornish saint, who was born in Callington, Cornwall of a Cornish family.

His father Seyf was a powerful chieftain, and legend say he is thought to be grandfather to King Arthur. His mother was Gwen, sister of Nonna, who was the mother of St David, the patron saint of Wales.

Cuby became a monk living in a cell next to the well at Tregony and dedicated his life to study. He died 5.11.555.

The engraved bowl from the well at Duloe is now in the nearby church. In Llangibby-on-Usk is a carved stone dedicated to him, and also a church and well which was used for healing TB, scurvy and rheumatism. The Holy Isle on Anglesey is named after him.

This is a lovely well with a gentle, nurturing atmosphere as you sit inside on either of the benches inside the front section, to spend some time in quiet contemplation.

Location-SX241 579

From Liskeard take the B3251towards Looe. (The road passes St Keyne where there is another holy well-no 14) there is no parking near the well nor pavement so care should be taken. Park near the church you pass on your right. Opposite the cider place on your left about a half mile down the road is the well which is signposted and sits in a small clearing under the trees.

There is a stone circle nearby in Duloe, opposite the church. There is a sign-posted path and across the field is the smallest circle in Cornwall, with only 8 stones. This is a place that comes alive at the time of the full moon. For many years there has been a ginger cat that escorts you to the circle and will often remain during your visit.

9- Dupath Holy Well

9-Dupath Holy well

There is no dedication to a particular saint associated with this well.

Legend says this was the site of a duel between a poor knight called Colan and a rich man Gottlieb for the hand of a maiden, but both died- Gottlieb in the dual and Colan soon after from his injuries.

Inside the large chapel of this stunning building, there is a plaque which says that the well was used for healing in the past, especially whooping cough in children, and may also have been used for baptism.

Like St Clether this chapel has a channel running through it to a bowl on the outside where the holy water can be collected.

Location-SX374 693

From Callington take the A388 towards Saltash. After about 2 miles there is a road on the left with a sign to the Holy well. Follow the road and take the track to the right which leads to a farm ahead. The well stands in a small fenced enclosure and there is parking provided behind a barn.

"Sometimes it seems the Fates have the control, that our free will has vanished like a puff of smoke. Keep the faith because sometimes there are greater forces at work than we can be aware of"

10- St Just Holy Well

10-St Just Holy well

Joseph of Arimathea supposedly landed here with Jesus when he was a boy about 10 or 12years of age, when they were travelling to Glastonbury to study.

This is a sweet little well, sometimes prone to flooding in severe weather conditions. Just being near you can feel the gentleness of it.

St Just was the son of St Geraint whose history in Cornwall can be traced through several generations and possibly included Sir Geraint of Round Table fame, though this might be a different line of the family history.

Location- SW848 356

From the A390 from St Austell take a left marked Tregony /St Mawes, then just past Trewithian is the A3078 to St Just in Roseland (not to be confused with St Just near Lands End) Take the turning signposted to St Just church.

When you enter the north gate a curved path will lead down to the church. Follow the path, past the church on the south side and follow around the bay. The well is on the right in the bank. There is a large stone cross near the church and one of the loveliest settings for a well in Cornwall, right on the estuary.

11- St Guron Holy Well

11-St Guron Holy well

He was also known as St Goran. He gave shelter to St Petroc and three of his friends from Padstow, where Petroc had his missionary. The story goes that he set the table with food for them and then vanished. He went to Gorran Haven to be a hermit and left St Petroc with the church in Bodmin.

Petroc ended his days as a hermit on Bodmin Moor. His body was returned to Padstow but the monastery was burnt by the Danes in 981 and his remains once again returned to Bodmin. His remains, his staff and saint's bell, lie in the church there.

 In the 9th or 10th century monks brought the gospels from Brittany including the only surviving manuscript from a Cornish Monastery recording the liberation of Cornish slaves from their Saxon owners.

Location-SX075 670

 Take the A388 into Bodmin and you will come to a large imposing church on the right. This is St Petroc's church, and next to the west wall is the well house of St Guron's well, with a carving of him in a niche above the (locked) door. Unfortunately he has now lost his head- maybe to demonstrate his eventual fate?

The water flows down to the foot of the church on the street corner, once the town centre. The water flows out of two gargoyle heads into the trough underneath, and would be used by animals and people alike to drink from.

"I try to be aware of the needs of the people who come to me for guidance but my time is running out. My spirit demands I retreat into solitude for contemplation and prayer. I leave you in the care of another."

12-St John's Holy Well-

12- St John Holy well

This well is dedicated to St John the Baptist.

He had baptised Jesus and foretold of his coming and greatness, to be the leader of men.

Location-SX291 714

From the B3254 between Liskeard and Launceston, take a turning to Pensilva. Go through the village and turn left at the pub on the left. Follow signs to Caradon Town and just before the turning into the hamlet is a fenced off triangle area. In here is a pond and the well of St John. The area is boggy and overgrown but the well has clear running water and a gentle atmosphere envelops the whole place.

"I beg you be still. Take time each day to sit in contemplation and meditation. Let the body and mind be at rest for a while and you will reap the rewards"

13-St James Holy Well

13-St James Holy well

St James was a companion of St Samson. (see no.30)

The water was often used for healing eye problems.

This is a beautiful well standing in a clearing with ivy, flowers and ferns growing all over it.

A very comforting place to curl up inside, and dream.

Location- SX091 769

From the A30 turn off for St Breward, or approach from the B3266. Park near the primary school and take the public path which drops down to the woods below. The well is in a small clearing looking quite beautiful in this special setting. It's a pity the well is now dry

"I am always looking for signs that will guide me in my decisions. Sometimes they are not easy to see, or maybe I don't look closely enough. I do know that I have never been let down yet"

14- St Keyne Holy Well

14-St Keyne Holy well

Feast day 8ᵗʰ October.

St Keyne was one of the daughters of King Brychen. She was known for her purity and beauty but also as quite eccentric......

She was a traveller, who then became a recluse and quite evangelical, trying to enrol anyone who passed her place of worship. She planted four of the Celtic sacred trees (Oak, Elm Ash and Willow) around the well. She was a powerful woman who was in tune with the old ways, as one story sometimes told, was said she could turn snakes to stone.

In later years the legend grew about her, that the first partner to drink from the well waters would rule the marriage, so to be sure when she married, she took a cup of water to the church to drink as soon as the union was made....(and her husband ran to the well for his cup of the magic waters). There is a carved plaque with the poem about this near the well which was put up when the well was restored in 1932.

Location-SX248 603

From Liskeard head towards the railway station and continue on the B3254 towards St Keyne. The road at the end of the village is a Y junction so take the left fork and the well is a little way down at the next turning on the left. The well is just on the roadside with steps from either side leading down to the well.

15-St Levan Holy Well

15-St Levan Holy well

Feast day= 18th November

He is also known as Selvan which means 'Solomon'. He is the father of St Cuby/Cybi (whose well can be found at Duloe and Tregony). He was a Cornish warrior prince in the 5th century and brother of St Just.

In the churchyard there is a huge rock which he is said to have struck and caused a crack to appear. The legend says- 'If ever the rock should split apart, enough for a horse to ride through- it will be the end of the world'.

He was known for curing toothache and sore eyes. His well was considered to be 'An eye on the face of Mother Earth'.

Location- SW381 219

Take the B3315 and turn off to Porthcurno and continue on to St Levan. There is a car park in a field next to the church to park.

Take the path from the side of St Levan church towards the beach at Porth Chapel. Follow the south west coast path, across a stream and the remains of the well are on the left just above the cove in a most remarkable setting. The chapel is a bit further along the path cut into the hillside. It is also possible to approach from The Minack side of the path.

16- St Mawes Holy Well

16-St Mawes Holy well

Feast day=6th February

He is said to come from South Wales, and is also known in Brittany where he was famed for curing snakebites. There are 60 Breton churches commemorating him.

He became a recluse and hermit, and the story is he carved a chair out of the rock above the well house, to use for meditation.

He was a teacher to Saint Budoc who has St Budeaux in Plymouth named after him. The chapel has vanished along with his shrine. This well is lacking any energy or atmosphere maybe due to its present setting and the locked door to the well.

Location- SW847 332

Take the A3078 from Tregony to St Mawes on the Roseland Peninsular. Park along Tredenham Road and make for the Victory Inn, which is on the front. To the left is a set of steps and at the top of these is the well, set into the wall of a garden in front of you.

'We need to be cautious about the things we waste, whether it be love, friendship, food or energy. We are all part of the 'whole'

17-Menacuddle Holy Well

17-Menacuddle Holy well

This well is dedicated to St Guidel who has a parish in Brittany. Nothing much is known about her, another history where records and stories have been lost or destroyed.

In 1250 the well name was spelt Menaquidel.

<u>Location- SX013 535</u>

From the town take the B3274 Bodmin Road towards Bugle and Roche. Go under the viaduct and a few yards further on is a slip road on the left. It has a sign for elderly people just before the turn as there is a residential home further on up this road. On your right is a grassy meadow, a stream and the most beautiful well tucked under the trees on the far side. Sometimes the waters flow white with the clay from nearby quarries and the waterfall sparkles as it makes its way down the valley.

This well was restored in 1922 by Sir Charles Sawle, in memory of his only son who died in the war. The well house has two arched doorways and a small window. The back wall is built into the granite wall behind, and the water springs from there into a basin inside.

"*Come –bring your children to me. I will heal them and bring comfort to them. Let them lie in my waters and all disease will flow away with the current.*

I will also bring comfort to those who look for love and guidance. Your most precious secrets are safe with me. Speak your wishes and listen well"

18- St Stephen Holy well

18-St Stephen Holy well

St Stephen was stoned to death when he was only 24 years of age, and so became one of the first Christian martyrs.

Paintings and manuscripts always show him with 3 stones about his person.

Location- SX320 857

Travel to Launceston and go down the B3254 which runs past the castle towards Newport. Over the bridge and bear left at the Y junction towards St Stephen church. Directly opposite is a road- Duke Lane. Park here and follow the footpath on the right towards Newhouse and the well is in front of you on the right.

'Not everyone will share your beliefs, so follow your own path, listen to your heart and proceed without fear'

19- St Michael Holy Well

19-St Michael Holy well

St Michael, like archangel Michael, is one of the 'greats', and renowned as 'The Protector' with his powerful sword to defend where needed.

There are several places in Cornwall dedicated to him including Rame chapel, Rough Tor where there are the remains of a chapel, and St Michael's Mount. There are many dedications to him all over Europe also.

Location-SX081 788

From the A399 between Wadebridge and Camelford, take the turning to Michaelstow and make for the church.

This well is to the right of the front door of the church, at the end of a small curved path. The water has been diverted to the farm behind the churchyard, so the well is now dry, and was full of dead leaves when I visited giving it an air of neglect and sadness.

'Be not afraid, I am always by your side'

RESTORED in 1862

20-St Neot Holy well

20-St Neot Holy well

Feast day-31st July.

St Neot studied at Glastonbury for several years and then moved to Cornwall to be a hermit.

He has another well dedicated to him at Poundstock.

This is a well which was used for healing children.

The well was previously dedicated to St Gueyer, who lived a very Spartan life, taking cold baths daily. (Maybe they are the same person and the stories have been mixed up?)

St Neot was passionate about the environment, used only what he needed, and would get angry about any unjustified waste. There is also a story that he had a deer as a companion.

His remains were stolen and taken to the new priory at Eynesbury where a new town called St Neot was founded with the agreement of King Edgar and the local bishop. A band of Cornishmen tried unsuccessfully to bring the remains back to Cornwall

Location- SX183 681

From the A30 between Bodmin and Liskeard take the turning to St Neot, a small village on the edge of Bodmin Moor. Park next to the church or by the pub. Alongside the pub is a track alongside a stream leading into an open meadow. The well is ahead of you built into the bank. The wooden well door opens onto a lovely well of clear water.

21- St Non Holy well

21-St Non Holy well

Feast day 15th June

St Non/Nonna, is the mother of St David (also known as Dewi Sant) the patron saint of Wales. The name Pelynt comes from Plou Nent– the parish of Non.

The chapel has now gone from above the well. There was a well dedicated to her at St Mawgan in Pydar. She died in Brittany and her tomb can be found at Dirinon, east of Brest.

 She is a powerful saint who is also known for her Moon magic.

This is a piskie well guarded by an elf that will follow you and cause much mischief if offerings were not left at the well. Also used for divining by dropping pins into the water. There is a story of a farmer who took the bowl from the well for his cattle and the next day it was back at the well. On the third time it was removed and again returned to its proper place the farmer was the target of much misfortune and went mad.

Location–SX224 564

On the B3359 just before Pelynt take the minor road east to Muchlarnick. Just before Sowdens bridge, walk up Hobbs Lane and the well can be found about 20 yards along the lane on the right under the hedge. The owners have repaired the site and put in steps and a handrail, so access to the well is much safer and easier. The well basin is beautifully carved and covered in moss and lichen and does feel like a place that the fairy folk would dwell.

22- St Kew Holy Well

22-St Kew Holy well

Feast day 8th January

She is also known as St Kewe or Kewa. St Kew is known as the patron saint of lost things, so if you need her help to locate something– sit with the card and ask her for help.

The village was previously known as Lan Docco or Landoho, after the monastery that stood here once. St Kew is the sister of Docco and worked with him in his missionary. Until the 15th century a chapel stood outside the church dedicated to St Kew, but was destroyed after alterations to the church building.

Location– SX023 768–

From the A39 between Wadebridge and Camelford take a turning at St Kew Highway into the village. The church is quite large and impressive for such a small hamlet. The locals have recently fundraised a large sum of money to replace one of the large windows,

The well can be found in the garden of the rectory. From the car park at the church walk to the left and the rectory is on your right. Just inside the wall surrounding the garden, the well can be found in the top left corner. The wooden door has recently been replaced and there is a cross erected above. The well was lost for a while until the vicar had it rebuilt in the 1890's.

"My brother is my life and work companion. He shares my dreams and I his goals to bring the people to the gift of Christianity and this is our mission"

23- St Julian Holy Well

23-St Julian Holy well

Julian and Julitta may be the same person. Sometimes the gender and the stories get confused especially as so many were not written until many years after the events. One story associated with him is he was fated to kill his parents. He is another of the children of King Brychen of Wales.

The well house was restored in 1882 by the Earl of Mount Edgecombe and measures 6ft x 4ft. There are niches for shrines but the water levels are almost nonexistent which is a pity, as this is a perfect place for travellers to take some rest as they cross from Devon into Cornwall.

Location –SX447 521

From the A38 at Trerulefoot turn onto the B3247 to Torpoint After a few miles there is a turning to the right to Millbrook and Cremyl. Continue on this road towards Cremyl and just past Maker church, on the right is the first entrance to Mount Edgecombe estate. Just a little way past this there is an arched drinking basin on the road, and the well is up a short path and steps up the bank behind the font.

"I have travelled from far distant places and I am bone weary. I need a place to drink, eat and rest my horse and myself, before I go any further. Life seems a burden to me at times and I can't overcome some of the thoughts that intrude on my dreams"

24-Jesus Holy Well

24-Jesus Holy well

A well for women's healing and whooping cough in children. The well house was repaired in 1952. It is called the Jesus well as it was a place he visited on his journey through Cornwall with Joseph of Arimathea.

The crew from the ship needed water and went inland to look for it. The ground was struck with a staff and a spring sprang up to provide pure clear water. Jesus holy well was covered in sand from the dunes for many years as was St Enodoc church (hence the leaning church tower) until it was restored.

Location- SW937 764

From the A39 take the B3314 to St Minver/ Pityme and follow the road on to Rock. Past the PO on the left, take 3rd turning on the right- Green Lane to the T junction. Park here and follow the footpath in front of you onto the golf course and the well is only a few yards from the path.

The well is in a small dip to protect it from the elements and possibly flying golf balls.

"I have listened to the cries of children and will help them with my curative waters which carry my healing and loving thoughts. Beware those who would take the gifts and offerings of the afflicted"

25- Roughtor Holy Well

25-Roughtor Holy well

This well is dedicated to St Michael. There are the remains of old settlements all around the area, and a faint memory of St Michael chapel.

<u>Location– SX147 810</u>

From the A39 between Wadebridge and Bude, stop at Camelford and take the turning to RoughTor, along a straight road to the car park. You will see the hills in front of you with Rough Tor to the right and little Tor on the left. The track across the moor leads you to the dip between the two. The well is about 2 thirds of the way up on the right and can be hidden by grasses and reeds. The well house is made of local granite with two large slabs over the roof. It was hard to get a sense of the size of the well due to overgrown vegetation and lots of water but when it was restored in 1994 was about 6ft long. The spring is clear but the area around is often wet and boggy, but that doesn't matter at all when you see the panorama of the moors around you.

There is a natural fogue under Rough Tor which is worth exploring.

"If this land could speak it would talk of hardships and strain, of stories from travelling men and women, of extremes in the weather patterns but most of all it speaks of our history and heritage"

27- St Piran Holy Well

26-St Piran Holy well

Feast day- 5th March

His name is sometimes spelt as Pirran or Perran also. He is the patron saint of Cornwall and of 'tinners' (the miners who dug for tin in the ancient earth of Cornwall) and on his feast day his life is celebrated at St Piran's Oratory on the north coast of Cornwall, just north of Perranporth. This is where his remains are buried and also a small copper bell, often used by missionaries to signal their arrival. This chapel has been covered by the sands on several occasions, the last in 1981, but has now been reclaimed. He died at the end of the 5th century.

There is another well dedicated to him at Perranarworthal. His first church was said to have been in Perranporth, but other places with a connection to him are Perranzabuloe, where his remains were kept and became a place of pilgrimage, and Perranuthnoe. He was a fifth century abbot, who may have come from Wales, but there is no definite information about this.

Location- SW779 388

On the B3263 between Boscastle and Tintagel there is a small car park on the roadside at Trethevy for those who wish to visit St Nectan's Glen. On the left just a few yards up the road to the turning is the well of St Piran, looking quite neglected and dejected. Turn right onto the track through the woods to the Kieve and take a moment to visit the small church on the left, previously dedicated to St Materiana. (a church in Tintagel is now dedicated to her).

"I once was a place for travellers from all ages to rest and drink my waters, bathe sore and tired feet and to wash away the dust of the road. I ring my bell at dusk each day so you can find me and take shelter"

27-Sancreed Holy Well

27-Sancreed Holy well/ Chapel Downs well

Feast day= 8th March

Although the well is known as Chapel Downs well and dedicated to St Euny, there is a St Sancreed who accidently killed his father. Through guilt and remorse, he became a hermit looking after pigs and started his ministry here.

This is a most spiritual and special place. The atmosphere around is palpable and one can imagine shape-shifters and other beings in one's presence, especially as you go down the several steps into the well- time and space seem to lose meaning.

Location- SW418 293

From the A3071, either from St Just or from Newbridge direction, there is a B road leading to Sancreed. Opposite the church there is a narrow path by the side of a house, which leads to the well- about ¼ mile walk.

The well itself is down a short flight of steps with room to stand inside. This is a very special well with healing powers and a great sense of mystery. Very near the well is a modern cross which seems at odds with the natural beauty of the

place. There are also the remains of the chapel walls nearby–
about 4ft high with several carved stones lying nearby.

28- St Crantocus Holy Well

28-St Crantock/ CrantocusHoly well

Crantocus is the son of Ceredig, and has links with monasteries and churches in Wales and Brittany.

The story associated with Saint Crantocus, is that King Arthur asked him to rid the land of a particular dragon who was causing trouble. Crantocus befriended the dragon, prevented the soldiers from killing it, tamed it and set it free. The dragon was no longer a danger to the local people.

Location– SW789 604

Crantock is on the south side of The Gannel River. From the A3095, turn left and follow signs to Crantock. The well is situated in a small walled area in the centre of the village, opposite the triangle green area. It is unusual in that it has a 'beehive' roof to the well house.

"Not everything is how it is presented. Consider how you use your time thinking and worrying which feeds the anxiety. Be still for a while every day."

29-Scarletts Well

29-Scarletts well

The well water is always 53 degrees at any time of year, and was famed for its healing powers. Stepping stones lead to the entrance of the well, as the run off to a small stream gets quite wet at certain times of the year.

The minerals in the water can appear to produce different colours in different lights and time of year.

Bodmin has a number of Holy wells, which shows how important a place it was once. All the wells can be found on one of the Town Trails, but several of them are neglected and lacking any presence.

Location- SX057 675

From Bodmin town centre, head out to the supermarket at the end of Berrycombe Hill, and the famous Bodmin Jail. (This is now a museum and restaurant. The cells are dank and harsh and creepy)

Scarletts Well Road runs along in front of the jail alongside the park area. At the end of this road is a track which leads directly to the well on your right.

30- St Sampson Holy Well

30-St Samson Holy well

Samson was born 490– 565. A lot has been written about his life and work as he was the founding father of the Breton church, leader and a political negotiator.

He was very active in converting people to Christianity, and quite passionate about it and very successful.

His father was Amon of Dyfed, his mother Anna of Gwent, who was thought to be barren, but then she had Samson who became a Healer, was known to cast out devils and raised a dead boy to life.

When he was ordained in 521 as bishop, fire was said to come from his nose and mouth and was used to defeat a giant serpent. He is also supposed to have tamed a troublesome witch in the area.

He travelled to Cornwall with his father Amon and landed at Padstow. From there he travelled to the monastery of Docco at St Kew. (Originally called Landocco which is the earliest recorded Cornish Monastery).

His gravestone is written in Latin and Irish Ogham.

One of the Isles of Scilly has been named after him. Other islands named after saints are– St Mary, St Martin, St Agnes, and St Helen.

<u>Location–SX121 551</u>

From the B3259 off the A390, at the crossroads with
Tywardreath (the scene of Daphne Du Maurier book– 'The
House on the Strand). Travel east to Golant and park near the
church. The well is tucked in on the left of the front entrance
to the church.

31-St Melor Holy well

31-St Melor Holy well

Sometimes his name is written as Mylor but this is the name of another Celtic saint. St Melor was decapitated in 411, and asked for his head to be put onto his staff, and from that a tree grew...

Location-SX319 732

Whichever way you go to Linkinhorne you will have to drive through winding lanes. From Callington take theA388 then turn onto the B3257, otherwise from Liskeard, take the B3254 towards Launceston and turn off at Upton Cross or Rilla Mill.

Park near the church and walk towards Browda. Over the second gate on the left, (the first leads into a farmyard) and down the left edge of the field and near the bottom you will come to a 'brow' in the landscape. Go over that wherever you can get through and the well is in a clearing just below on the left. The area was very muddy and overgrown but this was a nice well with clear water in the well and a friendly feel to it.

"We are all capable of transforming what we have into something new and fresh and of value to ourselves and

others. This can be thoughts, ideas, actions or behaviour so make a difference".

32- St Indract Holy Well

32-St Indract Holy well

(Sometimes called Chapel Farm well)

Not much is known about St Indract, except that he was a traveller throughout the south of the country.

Indract and his sister St Dominica were supposedly killed by robbers on the way to Glastonbury.

In a niche inside the well house is a statue of the virgin Mary (as at Ladywell in Botus Fleming nearby) The well has been restored and was rededicated in 1951.

Location– SX417 659

From Callington take the A388 towards Saltash. Take any turning to St Dominick and follow signs south to Halton Quay which overlooks the River Tamar, and is a beautiful spot to just watch and listen. Park at Chapel Farm and continue down the lane towards the river and the well is on the left about 100yards down.

"I travel the lands and meet so many folk who hold themselves close to their own. Children play and parents work hard to keep the home intact, so very important in these turbulent times. Look after each other well"

33-St Mary the virgin

33-St Mary Holy well

Mary the Virgin, Holy Mary Mother, Mary Magdalene etc. 'Mary' will always be a symbol of the female Goddess, whatever name she is given.

Location– SX405 614. Botus Fleming

From Callington take the A388 towards Saltash and turn off at Hatt. Or from the A38 from Liskeard to Saltash, turn off just after Landrake to Botus Fleming. Park near the church and walk east towards Moditonam Quay, near the school. Just at the first right turn the well nestles on the corner.

The well house has a niche at the back which holds the statue of the virgin. It is a pretty little well but not much energy exudes through the locked gates and it is quite dry now.

34- Veryan Holy Well

34-Veryan Holy well

(Veryan is another spelling of St Buryan. She was the daughter of Munster chief, and was known to heal paralysis. See 1-Alsia well)

Feast day 5th May

The church is dedicated to St Symphorian. Previously it was to the Celtic Saint Cybele, who was the saint associated with this area. She was a mountain goddess and patron of wild animals especially the hawk and the lion.

Symphorian refused to acknowledge her and changed the name and dedication.

The well can be found across the road from the church behind a heavy metal fence. It was in a very sorry state when I visited as it was full of rubbish and empty cans etc. This well was restored in 1912 and is now dry.

Location-SW515 407

From St Austell take the A390 towards Truro. Just past Probus take the A3078 towards St Mawes. Veryan is signposted on your left. Head into the village and to the church whose steeple can be clearly seen.

"As I stand looking out to the wild I call my guide animals to be with me on my journey. I am sad to be leaving friends and loved places behind but I must keep moving as long as I am able until I can find a new home and place to settle"

35-St George Holy Well

35-St George Holy well

Very little apart from a few stones on the stream bed, remain of the well. However, there is a strange blue hue to the steps leading over the stream, which runs right onto the edge of the beach of St George's Cove.

St George is the patron saint of England and according to some historians did not exist! He is usually depicted killing a dragon or serpent as the defender of a maiden, but as the serpent is often used as a symbol of the feminine, this might be giving mixed messages!

Location-SW918 765

From the A389 take the turning B3276 into Padstow town. Parking can be limited but there are usually places on the harbour area. Head towards the ferry landing stage but carry on along the south west coast cliff path towards Gun Point.

36- St Kenwyn Holy Well

36-St Kenwyn Holy well

Feast day 18th November

This is a well of Mother Earth, as once upon a time, you would have gone down the steps into the belly of the well, to taste the waters. Unfortunately the steps are covered by a locked metal grill so you can only peer through the vegetation into this special place, but the mystery of the saint still is palatable.

Kenwyn is thought by some to be an alternative name for Keyne (St Keyne-see 14)

Location- SW819 458

Truro. From the A390, Tregolls Road take the right into St Clement Street, then Pydar Street under the magnificent viaduct into Kenwyn Rd. Then turn right into Kenwyn Church Road. Park near the gate entrance and as you go into the gate the well is on your left.

"I am the true power of this place and all would bow before me. Come to me and I will nurture your soul. Drink my waters and I will quench your thirst for knowledge. Leave an offering and I will grant your desires"

37-St Keri Holy Well

37-St Keri Holy well

St Keri was one of the children of King Brychen. Her name can also be spelt as Ciara or Kira, and means friendship or virgin.

Not much is known about St Keri but Egloskerry means 'the church of Keria'

Location–SX272 865

From the A30 either head through Launceston and take a left to Egloskerry or continue to Kennards House and turn off there.

When you get to the village, park near the church. Just south of the church there is a new bungalow and a narrow rather overgrown footpath on the right, which leads down to a small field on the right, where the well lies. It may be overgrown with flowers and brambles and has a wooden gate over the opening, which can be easily removed to try the water and peer within.

"My family means so much to me, and growing up together meant that we could always be having fun until one of us had to move on to fulfil our own destiny. These memories are often in my thoughts"

38- St Eupius, Carn Brae Holy Well

38-St Euny / St Uny Holy well

Feast day= 1st February (one of the four major Celtic festivals– Imbolc)

St Euny is a very popular saint in Cornwall and there are several wells dedicated to him at– Sancreed, Lelant, and Wendron. (Merthry Euny well)

He is the patron saint of Redruth. His brother is St Erc (St Erth) and his sister is St Ia (St Ives) He was one of the Irish missionaries who landed at Hayle with Gwinear. He was martyred and at Wendron there is a church dedicated to Him.

Location–SW399 288

From the A30 take the A3047 for Redruth. Stay on this road which bypasses the town centre and after the fourth roundabout take a left to Carn Brae village. The hospital should be on your right. Park near the village hall and directly across the road is a grassy path that leads to the well, situated next to a small stream. The well has been cleared and a small plaque put up with the saints name on it.

The water is very pure and legend says that anyone baptised in it would not hang....

"In ancient times we worked with spirits of time and place. We worked with their energies for magic and healing. We were never refused as the spirits wished us well"

39- Pipewell

39-Pipewell

Liskeard- is also known as St Martin's well. The large church nearby is dedicated to him. St Martin was born in Hungary in 316 and was known as the soldier who gave half his cloak to a beggar. He had a dream some time later, that it was Christ wearing his cloak, and requested he be baptised. He later became a monk and then was Bishop of Tours.

The well previously had only three pipes and the middle one was the one with the most power for healing and divining. When the well was restored it then had four pipes and was re-named as Pipewell.

Location- SW649 253

This well is in the centre of town in Well Street just below Fore Street. For Liskeard leave the A38 and head to the town parking areas. The well is tucked by a charity shop next to the lane to Fore St. There are metal grills over the entrance and it is quite difficult to see the well trough inside the domed building.

The water is no longer suitable for drinking, we are told by a sign attached to the wall, and there is a sense of sadness about the well now, though at times I have felt the echo of its power.

40-Davidstow Holy well

40-Davidstow Holy well

Feast day= 1st March

Dedicated to St David, or sometimes known as Dewi, who lived in the 6th century, and died in 589.

St David was the son of Sant, King of Ceredigon and his mother was St Non/Nunna (Alternun and Pelynt have wells dedicated to her. See 58 and 21. She is buried in Brittany)

David is the patron saint of Wales. He supposedly lived on bread, vegetables and water only. There are nine dedications to him in Cornwall and seven in Brittany. The Vikings destroyed many of his monasteries in Wales but then after settling in the area, became Christian themselves and fought for the Welsh against the English.

The well was restored in 1871and is typical of most of the restoration work of that time, being quite solid and dense feeling.

The well house has a solid oak door and is quite large inside compared to some wells. The water was clear on my visit and reflected the coloured stones of the ceiling. There is an interesting large square stone above the entrance in the roof, with a hole carved into it. I could only speculate what its uses had been in the past. It is said that a lot of the stone and granite used came from nearby Lesneweth. The water was so pure it was used in the nearby creamery for the production of cheeses.

<u>Location– SX153 874</u>

From the A39, take the A395 and turn off for road to Davidstow. Park at the church, just to the right as you face the church is a path signposted Holy well. Follow the path across the field and over the small bridge and the well is in front of you. The ground can get quite boggy so wellingtons are suggested.

"As I stood at the entrance, I felt a sense of durability, of solidity. The values I try to live my life by, are the power of Love and Kindness which can move mountains, change lives and tribes and even countries."

41- St Nevet Holy well

41-St Nevet Holy well

St Nevet or Neva is the patron saint of Lanivet, and is the founder of Lannevet in Brittany.

Lanivet is near the centre point of the Saints Way, (the pilgrimage path across Cornwall from Padstow to Fowey which the Irish saints walked on their way to Brittany and France). Many years ago it was a major meeting centre for travellers and missionaries.

The church has several marked stones and one from the 6th century has the name ANNICU carved in to it. There is a 6th century pillar stone and twelve ancient crosses nearby which demonstrate the importance of the place.

Location-SW038 655

This well is on the side of the road at Hoopers Bridge. From Bodmin take the A389 towards St Austell. The garden nursery is on the left and then you are out of the dip and half way up the hill on the right is a turning for Nanstallon, take that and the first turn left which will bring you to the tiny bridge near Treningle.

"We are all travelling on our journey. My journey has been one of the spirit, and I was called when quite young, to take my place alongside other searchers. Come take rest from your travels and share stories with others who also go this way"

42-St Paternus Holy well,

42-St Paternus Holy well

Feast day= 7th April

St Paternus/ St Pattern- lived like a hermit, as did his father, until he was called by St Sampson (who has a well at Golant, see no.30) to follow his missionary.

He was accused of stealing, and to prove his innocence plunged his hand into boiling water, but it came out unharmed.

There are other stories associated with him and his links with Brittany, setting up a monastery at Vannes. He was a local chieftain whose son was St Constantine, who is celebrated with a well and chapel which lie on a golf course on the north coast of Cornwall.

Location- SX283 898

From the B3292 from Launceston towards Bude, and turn off for North Petherwin. Park near the church and take the public footpath east through the gate on the right and cross next two fields (there is a worn path skirting the field) If there are cattle the electric fence will be on so take care. At the end of the second field on the right, tucked under the hedge is the well of St Paternus.

Unfortunately it had a rather crude padlocked, metal gate over the entrance which affects the energy of the place. This is one of several holy wells that were restored by North Cornwall Council.

43-Stara Woods well

43-Stara Woods well

This is not a 'Holy well' as it has no dedication to any saint or legend. I have included it though as it is a beautiful and gentle well in a lovely setting which has a restful presence about it.

There are many such wells in Cornwall which are used as a water source for small communities and hamlets, and might once have a story or local legend which is now lost in time. I thought this little well might have healing properties, because when I put the water on a sore skin injury it felt better after only 15 minutes.

The woods where this well can be found, is a community resource and managed by volunteers.

Location–SX289 733

From Liskeard take the B3254 towards Launceston. Just past Upton Cross you come to Darley Ford and a sharp bend to the right. Continue up here to the right turning marked' Lower Lake shooting grounds' and continue down the road until you reach Stara Bridge at Rilla Mill, Near Liskeard. There is a small parking area on the left. Walk through the gate and follow the path along the river until you reach a fork in the path where you take the right path and the well is 20 yards on the right.

44-St Swithins Holy well

44-St Swithins Holy well

Feast day= 15th July

There is a legend that says that- if it rains on that day, (his feast day) it will rain for the next 40 days. His emblem is raindrops and apples.

He was said to have made whole again, the broken eggs of an old lady who had stumbled and dropped them.

He died 2.7.862 and his remains were moved again on 15.7.1971

Location-SS244 057

From Stratton take the A3072 towards Holsworthy and take the turn off to Launcells. When you get to the village head for the church, which is quite large and imposing for such a small place. The well is directly opposite the front entrance of the church, fenced off from the road but easily accessible. The little passageway to the well can get overgrown at times but once through the well is small and neat and the water is pure.

"People often have expectations of others, situations and circumstances. This is a trap we must be vigilant not to fall into. It is important to look at the other side of things before drawing a conclusion and acting irrationally or without the full facts."

45-St Genny Holy wells

45-St Genny Holy well

Feast day= 2nd May

St Genny is sometimes confused with the Roman soldier St Genesius, who was beheaded in 250 AD and whose feast day is on 25th August. Genesius has strong connections to Arles, in Provence in France.

It is possible that St Genny came from Wales and was brought here by the monks of Docco who built a church in the area, and had a large missionary at St Kew.

Location- SX149 971

From the A39 at Wainhouse Corner, take the road signposted to Crackington Haven. There are two wells here dedicated to Saint Genny. One is at the rear of the church with an arched wooden door. The other is in the bank under the road before the church. It is now in a private garden but easily visible as the area has now been cleared.

"We all pretend to be what we are not at times. This may be for recognition, love, glory or acceptance. It can also be because of fear- you must chose."

46-Jordans Holy well,

46-Jordans Holy well

St Sidwell –Feast day is 2nd August

The church is dedicated to St Sidwell, (maybe also known as St Sitifolla)

Side –fulle means 'full of light'. The cathedral in Exeter also celebrates this saint as she is buried there at the East Gate.

She was a Harvest goddess. There is a story that she was murdered, on the orders of her stepmother, with a scythe. (In pictures she is always shown with corn rood screens and a scythe)

Her brother was Paul Aurelon/or Paul of Mousehole who took 12 saints from Wales to Cornwall and then onto Brittany where he set up a monastery at St Pol de Leon.

Location– SX229 839

From the A395 between Davidstow and Kennards House, take the turning to Laneast. Towards the west of the church is a short lane leading to a group of houses with a track behind and a gate into a field, and the well is half way down surrounded by a fenced enclosure to keep out cattle.

"I am a beacon and draw others to me. I require you to shine with inner glow and happiness whenever possible. The light will bring peace."

47-Madron Holy well

47-Madron Holy well

Feast day= 18th November

The church is dedicated to St Madernus whose feast day is 17th May. There is some mystery about St Madron as he could have come from Wales (St Padarn) or have been the Irish Saint Madran.

It became Maddern in Europe, Asia, Africa and South America where 'clouties' are still used for healing at sacred places.

This is a well for healing and divination as young girls try to determine who and when they will marry.

Location-SW446 328

Just before Penzance on the A30 take a turning for Madron on the Morvah road. Go through the village and there is now a parking area near Boswarthen and a signposted path to the well and Baptistry. The Holy well of Madron is lost in undergrowth and mud but the hawthorn tree at the entrance to the area bears witness to its healing powers, as it is festooned with 'clouties'. These are rags or ribbons which are tied to the tree to bring about healing as they rot down.

Further along the path on the right is the baptistery which has its own water, an altar and stone benches within its walls.

The water here also has healing powers and it is a special place to commune with nature, the magic of past times and to make wishes. In 1641 the Bishop of Exeter examined a case of a boy who could only crawl for 16 years and then after sleeping in front of the altar, and washing in the stream three times was fully restored to health and mobility. He later enlisted in the army but was killed in Dorset in 1644.

There is a movement to restore the well but this is not certain. Madron was the Mother Church of Penzance.

48-St Julitta Holy well

48-St Julitta Holy well

Feast day– 16th June

St Julitta has churches dedicated to her at Luxulyan and St Veep. At Tintagel the chapel has a 12th century granite altar and there are twin Holy wells nearby. The chapel was known to be in use up to 1200.

Her church at Boscastle was restored by the novelist Thomas Hardy.

St Julitta was one of the children of King Brychan and known for healing skin diseases.

Her son Quricos was killed in front of her when only 3 years of age. She was tortured but did not weep, but welcomed him to martyrdom. Both bodies were rescued and buried together.

A gold necklace/circlet was found at the well and is now in the British Museum.

Location– SX093 829

From the A39 at Camelford take a turning on the right to the B3263 heading east out of the village. You come to a camping park just before Lanteglos called St Julitta Holiday Park. The well is through the site heading south, past the fishing lake on the right and tucked into a small clearing in a wooded area, with a huge protective tree standing sentinel nearby.

This is such a neat little well perched perfectly in the bank in this lovely setting and it was easy to forget what lay in the area above with lots of tourists and one has to wonder how many take the trouble to come and just sit in this special place.

"None can know the power of a protective symbol. I have such a small piece of stone that I carry constantly, that gives me comfort and quenches my thirst, and will keep me safe. None can hurt me"

49-Trezance Holy well,

49-Trezance Holy well

This is such a special well as you, and several others can stand inside.

The church in the village of Cardinham is dedicated to *St Meubred, (whose feast day is 20th May)*, who was a hermit from Ireland.

In the churchyard there are 2 inscribed stones from 6th and 7th centuries. Meubred can be seen with St Mabyn in one of the windows at St Neot church. He supposedly had his head cut off but was able to carry it around under his arm.

Location– SX125 694

This well can be located from the A30 between Bodmin and Bolventor (Jamaica Inn which stands here on the edge of the moor is the title of a Daphne du Maurier story) Take a turning signposted to Cardinham. You can also approach from the A38 between Liskeard and Bodmin– but be warned it is easy to get lost in the myriad of small lanes and many turnings and a definite lack of signposts.

The well itself is about a half mile from the church to the north. Park at the entrance to Trezance Farm (there is a new bungalow on the left. Head down the road and a few yards on the left is a row of stepping stones leading right into the well. It gets very wet so wellingtons are needed; otherwise just let the mud and cool waters ooze through your toes. The well is set into a bank and from above cannot be seen. This is a beautiful and magic place.

50-St Nectan

50-St Nectan

Feast day= 17th June

This is not a true well but a Kieve where Nectan had a meditation cave/chapel above the falls. It is still possible to sit in the cave for prayer and meditation and many offerings have been left as a token to this special and wonderful place.

Also known as St Nighton, he was the eldest son of King Brychen. There is a chapel near Lostwithiel dedicated to him, as well as chapels dedicated to him in St Winnow, Ashcombe and Chumleigh in Devon.

He landed in Devon at Hartland Point and was a hermit there in the forest, where he was buried after being killed by cattle rustlers. His church at Stoke held his shrine and pastoral staff.

His head was cut off by robbers and he was said to carry it around under his arm. People who can do this are called a cephalophore.

Location-SX083 884

Park in the allocated car park on the B3263 between Boscastle and Tintagel at Trethevy. (See St Piran Holy well no-26)

It is about 3/4rs of a mile walk through the woods until you reach the Glen where the waterfall is. There is a cave where he meditated and to stand in the pool under the falls is a truly magical and special experience which seems to bring alive the magic and mystery of the place. This is an essential place to visit to feed the spirit and find peace for the soul.

The water from the stream, at one time ran down through Rocky Valley to the sea. There are ancient labyrinth carvings on the walls along the valley.

51-Fenton Luna- Well of the Moon

51-Fenton Luna- well of the Moon

Unfortunately there is not much atmosphere to this well.

There is nothing left of the original well house, just an alcove in the boundary wall with a pump to represent the well and spring. There are writings which say that this is the true Holy well of Padstow but it is difficult to confirm with any certainty.

Location- SW915 755

Fenton Luna Lane, Prideaux Place, Padstow. The road is quite narrow but you can drive along it. The well pump is set in a small alcove of the boundary wall.

"At the cycles of the moon- waxing, waning and full, drink my waters and be sky clad, to celebrate the cycles of your life. The Moon affects us all to varying degrees and needs the respect and celebration it deserves, as it controls seas and rhythms of the planet and the body"

52-St Tremayne Holy well.

52-St Tremayne Holy well

Feast day= 4th June

Not much is known about this obscure saint but one of the local Cornish families is called Tremaine so the well could be connected and named after them.

<u>Location-SX162 969</u>

From the A39 take the road from Wainhouse Corner towards Crackington Haven. This road goes through the small hamlet of Coxford. At the cross roads head north and the well is on the side of the road. The well house was restored in 2000 and a seat added at the side. A lovely gift so that folk can sit in contemplation of the atmosphere of the well which contained several goldfish when I visited.

"Nothing is truly 'lost'. We misplace things or store them away until needed again. Knowledge too is never lost, it is absorbed, processed, changed and then manifests in a different form. No experience is ever wasted"

53-St Ia Holy well

53-St Ia Holy well

Feast day=3rd February

St Ia was an Irish saint, who is supposed to have travelled to Cornwall in a leaf (possibly a conical boat- the currach, used for fishing at that time)

Her two brothers Erc (424-514) and Euny (patron saint of Redruth) also came to Cornwall.

Another story is that she was the Irish daughter of a chieftain and came to Cornwall with a group led by Gwinear (*whose feast day is 23rd March*)- a very famous leader of the time, who was killed after he landed at Hayle in 450, by King Tewrig of Trencrom.

Some say she was killed at the same time, and others that she found protection from a local chief called Dinan, who built a church for her on the place where the well is today. It is possible that the female saint was Piala, the sister of Gwinear, who settled at Hayle. (There is a well and church dedicated to her there)

The well was used as a water supply until 1843 according to a sign above the well.

St Ives. The well is to be found above Porthmeor Beach, opposite the car park below Tate St Ives and the graveyard. It consists of two recesses in a granite wall in a cobbled area surrounded by a low wall

"I am the goddess of the fruits of the land. I provide sustenance and foods for you all especially the little children. Eat and be merry"

54-St Petroc Holy well.

54-St Petroc Holy well

Feast day– 4th June

Petroc was an abbot in the 6th century and a powerful Celtic saint. There are dedications to him in Somerset, Wales, Brittany and Devon as well as Cornwall.

He was a Welsh prince who studied in Ireland and sailed to Padstow where he set up his missionary. He had a little cell at Little Petherick which means 'Petrocs little homestead' Many said they saw him standing in the River Camel up to his neck, chanting psalms and prayers.

He was uncle to St Cadoc who has a well at Harlyn Bay, near Padstow.

He made pilgrimages to Rome and Jerusalem and lived for a while on an island in the Indian Ocean. He retired to live in a hermitage on Bodmin Moor. When he died his relics were buried at Padstow and then moved to Bodmin.

Location– SX076 667

The town can be reached from many directions but travel past the supermarket on the left and at the mini roundabout next to St Petroc's church, (the remains of an old monastery is at the rear of the church) turn left towards Lostwithiel. At the first set of lights turn left into Priory Park. Pass the pond on the left and go through to the next car park near the rugby club. Go to the far end and go down a grassy slope to a stream which is where the well is.

55-Rezare Holy well

55-Rezare Holy well

There is no specific saint associated with this well but it is obviously treasured by the community who maintain it.

There is a well dedicated to Saint Raze at Illogan– is this a connection?

The well is surrounded by a metal fence and the inside is gravelled and full of flowers in pots and troughs. The grill at the entrance to the well has a central cross in the design. The water is clear and the place is cared for and valued.

Location–SX362 775

From Callington take the A388 north towards Launceston. Travel past Stoke Climsland and Treburley then take the next turning on the right which will take you to Rezare. This well is at the centre of the village, outside Hope Farm.

"Spring is a time to rejoice as life reawakens after its slumbers. This time bids you to be active in your plans, to plant and to nurture your dreams to leave a lasting legacy for those to come"

56-Jacobstow Holy well

56-Jacobstow Holy well

This well is dedicated to St James, who sailed to France to set up his monastery which can be found on the pilgrim route to Compostella in Spain.

Location-SX191 963

From the A39 between Wainhouse Corner and Treskinnick Cross, there is a turning to Jacobstow. Before you reach the village there is a farm- Trefida, with a narrow track opposite leading to a gate. Then it is a walk across a field to a fenced area which is where the well is situated. We had to stomp through deep mud and boggy ground to reach it, and climb under barbed wire, but it was worth it. The well is set against a bank with curving walls leading to the entrance. The water was clear in the well but quite muddy at the entrance.

One feels a sense of history here in this place of journeying and visions.

57-St Morwenna Holy well

57-St Morwenna Holy well

Feast day= 8th July

Morwenna was one of the daughters of King Brychen of Wales.

It is said she built a chapel on the cliff side herself, carrying every rock and stone. Where she rested a spring appeared.

There is a story that when she was dying in the 6th century, she asked her brother St Nectan, to carry her to the well so she could look towards her Welsh homeland.

Location -SS197 155

Take the A39 northwards to the far western edge of North Cornwall and past Stratton and Bude is a turning for Mowenstowe. There is parking near the church but the well is on the Cliffside over two fields. It is only a narrow path to the well and is very dangerous– not for the faint hearted or someone scared of heights as the cliffs tower many, many feet above the bay. It is said ropes and tackle are needed now due to erosion.

To stand at the top of these cliffs one can get a sense of power and faith and commitment.

The church is famous for its rather eccentric vicar, R.S. Hawker who served during the 19th century. There is a statue in the grounds and inside the church commemorating him.

"Wherever we travel need a place to rest, to BE. I am at the edge of the world here, and spend many hours looking out to sea in quiet contemplation. I like my solitude which helps me get in touch with the goddess who rules the earth we all depend on."

58-St Nunna Holy well

58-St Nunna Holy well

Feast day-15th June

St Nunna/ Nonna/ Nun is the mother of St David, the patron saint of Wales. There are nine dedications to him in Cornwall.

Location- SX226 816

From the A30 between Launceston and Bolventor there is a turning to Alternun. (Which means- Non's altar) North of the church at Alternun, towards Trekennick, there is a double gate on the right (one for vehicles and the other pedestrian). This leads into a sloping field which was full of bullocks on my visit.

In the right bottom corner of the field is a walled and barbed wired area with a metal gate saying Holy Well. (This is locked so you need to scramble over the wall) There is a large stagnant pool and the area is very overgrown so it is difficult to get along the bank to the well house. This is a 'bowsenning' pool used for dowsing folk with emotional and mental problems, as at St Cleer.

It is tragic that a village that has won awards for 'best kept village' should neglect what could be a special place of pilgrimage and healing.

"In times of stress we are all vulnerable to base thoughts and fantasies which can affect us deeply. Bathe in my waters and you shall have respite and old grievances can be forgotten"

59- St Pratt Holy well

59- St Pratt Holy well

Feast day 11th September

St Pratt is thought to be an ancient Celtic saint, but before him the church was venerated to St Adwen.

St Pratt could possibly be a Roman martyr named Protus, who alongside Hyacinth was burned to death. The church is dedicated to Protus and Hyacinth together, and Protus also has the same feast day as St Pratt.

Location–SX104 732

From the A30 between Bodmin and Temple take the turning north for Blisland. In the village is a grassy area with an ancient Celtic cross. The well is set in the bank with a concrete channel which the water runs through.

"We make the most of every situation, to improve our life, develop our work or to help others. Doing things with a happy heart will make everything seem much better"

60-St Clement Holy well

60-St Clement Holy well

St Clement was passionate about education and set up a school for learning for young boys.

Location-SW853 438

Just before Truro on the A390, there is a sign on the left for Pencalenick which will lead to St Clement. Go down to the water's edge and park. Follow the path on the right for only a few yards and you will see the ancient well tucked in by the path. There is a real sense of the ancient history here and the presence of elementals.

There is also another well in the street before the river on the right- a small red brick building, again dedicated to St Clement but with a much more recent feel to it.

"I am the 'story teller' I can weave magic through words. Through words our imagination can fly. Come fly with me"

61-St Martin Holy Well

61-St Martin Holy well

St Martin was known for giving half his cloak to a beggar, to give him cover and keep him warm. (see Pipewell no. 39)

There are churches in Looe and Liskeard dedicated to him.

Location– SX258 524

The best way to approach this is from No Mans Land on the B3253. Go past the turning for Millendreath on the left, and head towards Looe. There is a turning on the left to Barbican which you take and Looe school is on the right. Next to the school is Sunrising estate which has a central square area. From there is a path leading towards Shutta past metal railings. As the path goes downward there is an area on the right, under the bank which is the site of the well. There is a metal fence around the well due to the fact that a child drowned there in the past. It was a rather forlorn place, maybe due to the tragedy, or the darkness and damp feeling. Not a place to linger but with some attention it could be made well again.

"For every action there will be a reaction or consequences as a result. Think carefully about what you do, and as far as possible do kindly by others, so there is no harm"

62-St Ruan Holy well

62-St Ruan Holy well

Feast day= 30th August

St Ruan was a monk who trained at Glastonbury. He was known for his love of all animals, especially wolves. There is a story that he was supposedly very hairy. The people were scared of him (and thought him a changeling) so cut his head off.

In the church is a stone figure of the saint.

(St Rumon is the saint buried at Ruan Lanihorne. St Ruan's remains lie in Tavistock)

Location-SW894 421

From the A390 turn off onto the A3078 and take the turning to Ruan Lanihorne. It can also be approached from Tregony on the B3287. You can park near the church and walk down the road in a westerly direction. The Shute from the well is on the roadside on the right. Look beyond and in the farm area you will see an arched building with a pool and stream running from it, which I took to be the well. It is quite lovely.

(St Ruan also has a well dedicated to him at Cadgwith on the Lizard, Location- SW716 147)

"Dreams are an awakening to many things. Work with your dreams and guides to help with understanding and personal growth. Do not just interpret through symbols but look deeper at the messages your guides are trying to convey"

63-St Mylor Holy well

63-St Mylor Holy well

St Mylor -1 possibly arrived in Cornwall from Brittany where he was an abbot-bishop and was known as St Meloir.

Mylor- 2 is the son of King Melianus of Cornwall whose uncle wanted to disinherit him and cut off his right hand and left foot, as in Celtic law, a maimed person was not allowed to rule.

The boy was brought up in a monastery and had metal limbs fitted. When his uncle learned of this he had him killed. Called Methyr Myle (Martyr Mylor) King Athelstan of Wessex gave his remains to Amesbury Abbey.

There are also dedications to him in Wiltshire.

Location-SW820 353

From the A39 travel through Truro towards Falmouth and take a left to Penryn on the B3292 and follow signs to Mylor Bridge. Park near the church on the quay and enter by the first gate on the right. The well is just inside on the right at the edge of the path towards the church. It is worth taking some time to visit the church which has some interesting features.

Appendix A ------ King Brychen-

Born in 490 and died in 550. His name means 'little badger'. His mother is Marcella, and according to the custom of the time, he was fostered with a wise man from four years of age.

According to the writings of St Nectan (the eldest son of Brychen), King Brychen was a 5th century King of South Wales. He married Gladwisa and is recorded as having fathered 24 children with her. The family moved to Cornwall and all of the children became saints and martyrs. Many of the names of towns and villages are taken from the children when they settled here. (Name given in brackets)

In the church at St Neot, on the edge of Bodmin Moor, there is a stained glass window showing him with several of his children.

Adwen= (Advent)
Cynog
Clether= (St Clether)
Endellient= (St Endellion)
Helie
Johannes (Sion) = (St Ives)
Iona
Juliana
Kenhender or Cynidr
Mabon= (St Maybyn)
Menfre or Menefrewy= (St Minver)

Merewenna/Morenna=Lamorran
Morwenna= (Morwenstow)
Nectanus= (St Nectan)
Tamalanc
Tedda/ Tetha= (St Teath)
Wencu
Wenheden= (St Enoder)
Wenset
Wynup
Yse = (Issey)
Keri= (Egloskerry)
Heli= (Egloshale)
Lanent=(Lelant)

Feast days of the Saints of the Holy Wells-

Town	Saint's name	Date of feast day
Altarnun	Saint Non	11th September
Blisland	Saint Pratt/ Praternus	7th April
Bodmin	Saint Goran	4th June
Cardinam	Saint Meubred	20th May
Cubert	Saint Cubert	12th December
Egloskerry	Saint Keri	2nd February
Laneast	St Sativola	5th May
Lanlivery	St Bryvyth	14th October
Lelant	St Euny	6th November
Luxulyan	St Suian	17th May
Madron	St Madron	18th November
Mawes	St Mawes	24th September
Mawgan	St Mawgan	24th September
Morwenstow	St Morwenna	18th October
Padstow	St Petroc	12th June
Perranworthal	St Piran	5th March
Roche	St Gonand	30th August
Lanihorne	St Ruan	30th August
St Buryan	Alsia	4th November
St Cleer	St Claire/ Cleer	4th November
St Clether	St Clether	13th November
St Gennys	St Genny	31st July
St Ives	St Ia	16th June
Kenwyn, Truro	St Kenwyn	18th November
St Kew	St Kew	8th October
St Keyne	St Keyne	25th June
St Levan	St Selevan	18th November
St Mawes	St Mawes	6th November
St Neot	st Neot	4th April

Trethevy	St Nectan	6th November
Sancreed	St Sancreed	8th March
Stithians	St Stediana	28th July
Tintagel	St Materiana	3rd March
Veryan	St Buryan	13th July

Appendix C ------ Oracle card meaning-

1	Alsia well	St Buryan	DESIRE
2	St Anne	Whitstone	BAPTISM
3	St Bryvyth	Lanlivery	MYSTERY
4	St Cleer	Nr Liskeard	CURES
5	St Clether	Nr Laneast	PEACE
6	St Cyors	Lanlivery	REMEMBERING
7	Chapel Euny	Carn Euny village	SACRED SPACE
8	St Cuby	Duloe	TRUST
9	Dupath	Callington	STRUGGLE
10	St Just	St Just in Roseland	WELCOME
11	St Guron	Bodmin	CHANGE
12	St John	Caradon Town	SILENCE
13	St James	St Breward	VISION
14	St Keyne	Liskeard	PURITY
15	St Levan	Nr Porthcurno	ENLIGHTENMENT
16	St Mawes	St Mawes	CAUTION
17	Menacuddle	St Austell	SAFETY
18	St Stephen	Launceston	TRILOGY
19	St Michael	Michaelstow	PROTECTION
20	St Neot	Liskeard	BALANCE
21	St Non	Pelynt	RESPECT
22	St Kew	St Kew Highway	UPLIFTING
23	St Julian	Maker	DESTINY
24	Jesus	Rock, St Minver	HEALING
25	Roughtor	Camelford	ANCESTORS
26	St Piran	Trethevy	REST
27	Sancreed	Nr St Just	VISIONS
28	Crantocus	Crantock	BUSY
29	Scarletts	Bodmin	COLOUR
30	St Samson	Golant	ACCEPTANCE
31	St Melor	Linkinhorne	TRANSFORMATION
32	St Indract	Halton Quay	FAMILY
33	Our Lady	Botus Fleming	FEMININE ENERGY

34	Veryan	Veryan	SADNESS
35	St George	Padstow	MISUNDERSTANDING
36	Kenwyn	Truro	RESTORATION
37	St Keri	Egloskerry	PLAY & FRIENDSHIP
38	St Eupius	Carn Brae village	FLOWING
39	Pipewell	Liskeard	EFFORT
40	St David	Davidstow	KINDNESS
41	St Nevet	Lanivet	CENTRE
42	St Paternus	Petherwin	SEARCHING
43	Stara Woods	Rilla Mill	COMMUNITY
44	St Swithan	Lancellos	MENDING
45	St Genny	Crackington Haven	CONTROL
46	Jordans well	Laneast	LIGHT
47	Madron	Madron	SECRETS
48	St Julitta	Lanteglos	CHARM
49	Trezance	Cardinham	DEPTH OF SECRET PLACES
50	St Nectans	Trethevy	WISDOM
51	Fenton Luna	Prideaux, Padstow	MOON ENERGY
52	St Tremayne	Coxford	HIDDEN TREASURE
53	St Ia	St Ives	ADVENTURE
54	St Petroc	Bodmin	CARE
55	Rezare	Nr Linkinhorne	CONTINUITY
56	St James	Jacobstow	THINKING
57	St Morwenna	Morwenstow	BUILDING
58	St Nunna	Alternun	FORGIVENESS
59	St Pratt	Blisland	LAUGHTER
60	St Clement	Falmouth	LEARNING
61	St Martin	Looe	CONSEQUENCES
62	St Ruan	Ruan Lanihorne	DREAMING
63	St Mylor	Mylor	SERENITY

Appendix D ------ Holy wells- Locations

1	Alsia well	St Buryan	SW393 251
2	St Anne	Whitstone	SX263 985
3	St Bryvyth	Lanlivery	SX078 590
4	St Cleer	Nr Liskeard	SX249 683
5	St Clether	Nr Laneast	SX203 847
6	St Cyors	Lanlivery	SX054 580
7	Chapel Euny	Carn Euny village	SW399 288
8	St Cuby	Duloe	SX241 579
9	Dupath	Callington	SX374 693
10	St Just	St Just in Roseland	SW849 358
11	St Guron	Bodmin	SX075 670
12	St John	Caradon Town	SX291 714
13	St James	St Breward	SX091 769
14	St Keyne	Liskeard	SX248 603
15	St Levan	Nr Porthcurno	SW381 219
16	St Mawes	St Mawes	SW847 332
17	Menacuddle	St Austell	SX013 535
18	St Stephen	Launceston	SX320 857
19	St Michael	Michaelstow	SX081 788
20	St Neot	Liskeard	SX183 681
21	St Non	Pelynt	SX224 564
22	St Kew	St Kew Highway	SX023 768
23	St Julian	Maker	SX447 521
24	Jesus	Rock, St Minver	SW937 764
25	Roughtor	Camelford	SX147 810
26	St Piran	Trethevy	SX076 892
27	Sancreed	Nr St Just	SW418 293
28	Crantocus	Crantock	SW789 604
29	Scarletts	Bodmin	SX057 675
30	St Samson	Golant	SX121 551
31	St Melor	Linkinhorne	SX319 732
32	St Indract	Halton Quay	SX417 659
33	Our Lady	Botus Fleming	SX229 839
34	Veryan	Veryan	SW515 407
35	St George	Padstow	SW918 765
36	Kenwyn	Truro	SW819 458

37	St Keri	Egloskerry	SX272 865
38	St Eupius	Carn Brae village	SX684 407
39	Pipewell	Liskeard	SW649 253
40	St David	Davidstow	SX153 874
41	St Nevet	Lanivet	SW038 655
42	St Paternus	Petherwin	SX283 898
43	Stara Woods	Rilla Mill	SX289 737
44	St Swithan	Lancellos	SS244 057
45	St Genny	Crackington Haven	Sx149 971
46	Jordans well/ St Sidwell	Laneast	SX229 839
47	Madron	Madron	SW446 328
48	St Julitta	Lanteglos	SX093 829
49	Trezance	Cardinham	SX125 694
50	St Nectans	Trethevy	SX885 085
51	Fenton Luna	Prideaux, Padstow	SW915 755
52	St Tremayne	Coxford	SX162 969
53	St Ia	St Ives	SW515 407
54	St Petroc	Bodmin	SXZ076 667
55	Rezare	Nr Linkinhorne	SX362 775
56	St James	Jacobstow	SX191 963
57	St Morwenna	Morwenstow	SS197 155
58	St Nunna	Alternun	SX226 816
59	St Pratt	Blisland	SX104 732
60	St Clement	Falmouth	SW853 438
61	St Martin	Looe	SX258 524
62	St Ruan	Ruan Lanihorne	SX894 421
63	St Mylor	Mylor	SX820 353

Appendix E ------ My Guide-

My guide on this journey has been one of the old pagan Goddesses. She has forgotten her given birth name after many years in retreats, closed orders, and nunneries, so now just goes by the name of Mary.

For many years she lived in a cave in west Cornwall growing what food she could and bartering for the rest by producing healing ointments and herbal drinks and potions. After many years living like this she was accepted into a monastery and did many solitary and silent retreats. She continued to grow herbs for medicines, making her cures and teaching others her skills. She probably lived in 3rd or 4th century.

I have loved every moment of this journey.......

Bibliography-

Ancient and Holy Wells of Cornwall- M & L Quiller- Couch. 1898

Secret Shrines- Paul Broadhurst. 1988

In Search of Cornwalls Holy Wells- Cheryl Straffon. 1998 and revised 2005

The Cornish Saints- Peter Beresford- Ellis. 1992

Echoes of The Goddess- Simon Brighton & Terry Welbourn. 2010

Pagan Cornwall- Cheryl Straffon. 1993

Celtic Saints, Passionate wanderers- Elizabeth Rees, 2000

Holy Wells- Phil Cope. 2010

Celtic Cornwall- Alan M. Kent. 2012

Holy Wells of Cornwall- A Lane-Davies. 1970

Cornwall and the Cross-Nicholas Orme. 2007

Biography-

I have lived and worked in Cornwall for over forty years.

For several years I taught Special Needs groups confidence building skills, before moving into Mental Health. Later I worked in Supported Housing for people with mental health issues or learning disabilities, teaching and encouraging independence.

I now have my own practice working as Master Reiki practitioner, and Reflexologist which I love. I have also trained in other Complimentary Therapies and continue to work at the cancer drop-in centre at my local hospital.

My interest in Holy Wells began several years ago when I set out to visit as many as possible, little knowing how many there are in Cornwall. So far I have visited over 200 but there are many more hidden away in special places in the landscape. This has been a journey of discovery and wonder, stimulating and interesting, and has developed my spiritual awareness and practices.

Contact HelenFox

helenfox@sifipublishing.co.uk

info@sifipublishing.co.uk

SIFIPUBLISHING

WWW.SIFIPUBLISHING.CO.UK